The N...
the Pan,
and the
Egg

Written by Pamela Gould
Illustrated by Randy Verougstraete

Scott Foresman

We see a big egg.

What can we do?

We can not fix the egg.

But the man can fix the egg.

"Where is my pan?

I can fix an egg in my pan."

The pan is yellow and big.

But the pan is not hot.

"I can get the pan hot!
Look at the hot pan!"

"Get a fan!

Fan the hot pan!"

We do not like the egg.

The egg is not yellow.

We can fix a ham.